DUCK UNDER THE TABLE!

More scenes from family life

Dear Tammie,
I hope you like
Australia as much as
we do since you've been
here.
Love from Colleen,
X-mas Down Under,
'93

Collected by Gwenda Beed Davey
Illustrated by Peter Viska

Melbourne
Oxford University Press
Oxford Auckland

OXFORD UNIVERSITY PRESS

Oxford New York Toronto
Delhi Bombay Calcutta Madras Karachi
Petaling Jaya Singapore Hong Kong Tokyo
Nairobi Dar es Salaam Cape Town
Melbourne Auckland
and associated companies in
Berlin Ibadan

OXFORD is a trade mark of Oxford University Press

First published 1991

National Library of Australia
Cataloguing-in-Publication data:

Davey, Gwenda.
Duck under the table!: more scenes from family life.

Includes index.
ISBN 0 19 553303 8.

1. Folkore — Australia — Juvenile literature. 2. Children's poetry, Australian. 3. Aphorisms and apothegms — Juvenile literature. I. Viska, Peter. II. Title.

398.80994

Typeset by Bookset, Melbourne
Printed in Australia by Impact Printing Victoria Pty Ltd
Published by Oxford University Press
253 Normanby Road, South Melbourne, Australia

Introduction

Duck Under The Table! is a sequel to my first collection of family sayings and rhymes, **Snug As A Bug!** For this book my sincere thanks go to the many listeners to ABC Radio's *Talking History* who wrote in for several weeks after my interview by Tim Bowden on that programme.

The rest of the items are from my own collection, and all the material is now housed in the Australian Children's Folklore Collection in the Melbourne University Archives.

A number of the rhymes and sayings are from languages other than English, and the index at the back of **Duck Under The Table!** indicates which language each has come from. The adaptations into English are my own, and I have used only items where the words and the spirit of the English are very close to the original. Everything in **Duck Under The Table!** has been collected in Australia.

To all the people who have shared these family treasures with me, thank you!

Gwenda Beed Davey

About the author

Gwenda Beed Davey is a respected authority on Australian folklore and has lectured in Australian Folklore Studies at the Institute for Early Childhood Development and elsewhere. She is co-editor, with Graham Seal, of *The Oxford Companion to Australian Folklore* which is due to be published in early 1993.

Gwenda traces her interest in household sayings back to her own childhood when her grandmother would complain of 'having a bone in her leg', and her father would say he 'was going to see a man about a dog'.

About the illustrator

Peter Viska is a well-known and much-loved animator and illustrator, mainly of children's books. His other projects include designing and illustrating stamps for the Australian Bicentenary and the International Year of Literacy. He also created the animated series *The Hedge and Mr Snip* and *The Greatest Tune on Earth* for the Australian Children's Television Foundation.

Peter is a father of four, and describes himself as an iconoclastic optimist for whom the early editions of *MAD* magazine were a profound influence. His fans will agree that beneath the cheeky deftness of his drawings is a keen understanding of children and their world.

Contents

FOOD

The nearer the bone the sweeter the meat.
All joints on the table will be carved!
The geese are flying.
Please.

It's raining, it's raining,
On mouse's wedding gown.
Her veil's made of silk,
But she's fallen in the milk,
And the cat's upside down.
Thank you.
Kiss my foot.

First come, first served.

I'm so hungry
I could eat a horse and chase the rider.

What won't fatten will fill.

If wishes were horses, beggars would ride.
You can't have your cake and eat it too.
V.

Fingers were made before forks.

What's that got to do with the price of eggs?

I've got a bone to pick with you.

One word's as good as ten,
All bog in,
Amen.

It's all a matter of taste,
as the old woman said
when she kissed the cow.

You haven't got a leg to stand on.
He's a lot of hot air.

Manners maketh man.
All the fine compliments,
All the best wishes,
Never replace
Help with the dishes.

Milk is binding,
So is cheese,
Eat fresh fruit
And work with ease.

Pardon me for being so rude,
It was not me it was my food.

Watch out, they'll go through you
like the Ballarat Express.

Past me teeth and over me tongue
Look out stomach, here I come.

You must have hollow legs.

What are you drinking, Mum?

Cow juice.

Roast, toast, frizzle or fry,
Make a pudding or bake a pie,
Melt in your mouth like butter,
Go down your throat like a railway engine
    going down a coal mine.

What's for dinner?

Sardines and custard.

Bread and scrape.

Prickly pears and sore fingers.

Bread and pullet.

What's for dinner?

Pickled eel's feet and geese's left eyebrows.

A large plate of wait and see.

Wait-and-see pudding.

What's for dinner?

Bread and butter and a duck under the table.

There were ten green bottles
Hanging on the wall,
Ten green bottles
Hanging on the wall,
And if one green bottle
Should accidentally fall,
There'd be nine green bottles
Hanging on the wall.

Nine green bottles
Hanging on the wall,
Nine green bottles
Hanging on the wall,
And if one green bottle
Should accidentally fall,
There'd be eight green bottles
Hanging on the wall.

Eight green bottles
Hanging on the wall,
Eight green bottles
Hanging on the wall,
And if one green bottle
Should accidentally fall,
There'd be seven green bottles
Hanging on the wall.

Seven green bottles
Hanging on the wall,
Seven green bottles
Hanging on the wall,
And if one green bottle
Should accidentally fall,
There'd be six green bottles
Hanging on the wall.

Six green bottles
Hanging on the wall,
Six green bottles
Hanging on the wall,
And if one green bottle
Should accidentally fall,
There'd be five green bottles
Hanging on the wall.

Five green bottles
Hanging on the wall,
Five green bottles
Hanging on the wall,
And if one green bottle
Should accidentally fall,
There'd be four green bottles
Hanging on the wall.

Four green bottles
Hanging on the wall,
Four green bottles
Hanging on the wall,
And if one green bottle
Should accidentally fall,
There'd be three green bottles
Hanging on the wall.

Three green bottles
Hanging on the wall,
Three green bottles
Hanging on the wall,
And if one green bottle
Should accidentally fall,
There'd be two green bottles
Hanging on the wall.

Two green bottles
Hanging on the wall,
Two green bottles
Hanging on the wall,
And if one green bottle
Should accidentally fall,
There'd be one green bottle
Hanging on the wall.

One green bottle
Hanging on the wall,
One green bottle
Hanging on the wall,
And if one green bottle
Should accidentally fall,
There'd be nothing but the smell
Hanging on the wall.

WORDS OF WISDOM

Your blood's worth bottling.
There's Sulky Sue, what shall we do?
Put her in the corner until she comes to.
You're a sight for sore eyes.
Sue

One two three four five six seven,
All good children go to heaven.

Your bladder's too close to your eyes.

You're like a bear with a sore head.

He's as flash as a rat
with a gold tooth.

You're as silly
as a two-bob watch.
Cat got your tongue?
You look as miserable
as a bandicoot.

You're like a bull in a china shop.

He's as crooked as a dog's hind leg.

All over the place like a dog's dinner.

As useless as a sore behind to a boundary rider.

You'd cut off your nose to spite your face.

He talks like a butcher's magpie.

Ah, the grubbo from Dubbo!
Hold your horses!
Bob's your uncle!

You got out of the wrong side of the bed!
You've got a bee in your bonnet!

You're making more noise than a walloping window blind.
You've been vaccinated with a gramophone needle.
I could talk to you till the cows come home.

He's running around
like a chook with its head chopped off.

Better than a slap in the belly with a wet fish.

Better than a poke in the eye with a burnt stick.

A sparrow in the hand
is better than a pigeon on the roof.

When my ship comes in.
Worse things happen at sea.

There's too many chiefs and
not enough Indians.
KA
VIS

Your lip would trip a duck.

I've got butterflies in my stomach.

You've got the collywobbles.

Feed a cold, starve a fever.

You look like something the cat dragged in.

You want to know the ins and outs of a duck's behind.
You can stew in your own juice.

She thinks she's the cat's whiskers.
Where's Dad?

He shot through like a Bourke Street bus.
How are we getting there?
Shank's pony.

It's like looking for a needle in a haystack.

Things are crook in Tallarook.

As scarce as hen's teeth.

I’ll be ready in two shakes of a lamb’s tail.

If brains were dynamite, you'd be safe.

Two heads are better than one,
even if they're only sheep's.

He's as happy as a sandboy.

I've got a bone in my leg.
I didn't come down in the last shower.
I wasn't born yesterday.

If it had been a dog it would have bitten you.
Little pitchers have long spouts.
You can't see the forest for the trees.

TV VIDEO
RENT/CEASE/BUY
NEW
LOOK
2

Between you and me and the doorpost.

I can see your poppy show,
All the way to Cottlesloe.

Have you heard the story about the three wells?
Well, well, well.

Beg your pardon,
Grant your grace;
Hope the cat
Will spit in your face.
You look like the cat
that's swallowed the canary.
I forgive you,
though thousands
wouldn't.

Do you know what?

What?

You’re mad and I’m not.

I'll kick you into the middle of next week.
I'll eat you raw.

I'll drop ya — like a mozzie on Mount Kozzie.
None of your shenanigans.
I'll come down on you like a ton of bricks.

Each to his fancy
and me to my Nancy,
said the old man as he kissed the cow.

Fischer's Fritz fishing for fresh fish.

My hand's itchy!
That means you're coming into money.

I'm flat out like a lizard drinking.

QUESTIONS

What's the time?

Half past a freckle with a mole catching up.

Time you got a watch.

Where are you going?
After my nose to show my tail the way.
What did your last slave die of?

Where are you going?
Up the river in a sardine jar.

Where's Mum?
In her skin — when she jumps out you can jump in.

Where's Mum?
Up the river shooting oysters.

Where's Dad?
Gone to Woop Woop.
NTH. WOOP
WOOP
STH. WOOP
WOOP WOOP

Where's Mum?
She ran away with a drunken sailor.
Where's my sports bag?

Up there hanging on a sky hook.

Where's my sock?
Up in Annie's room behind the clock.
Why?

Because Y’s a crooked letter and Z’s no better.

What do you want?
Well, take it and scram.
Nothing.
FIRST PRIZE
RAFFLE

What do you think this is? Bush week?
Money doesn't grow on trees.
PRODUCE
CAKES
JAMS
SHOW SPECIALS
FRESH

What's that?

A silver new nothing wrapped
in brown paper.

What are you looking for, Mum?
A horse feather and a run
around the yard.

Auntie Mary, Auntie Mary,
Lost the leg of her drawers:
Uncle Willy, Uncle Willy,
Will you lend me yours?

How far is it?
Twice as far as from here to there.

How much does that cost?
Money and fair words.
BOOKS
IN STOCK
REA
NEW

How much does that cost?
Twice as much as a half.
SOAP
BEST BUY
NOW EXTRA
BONUS

How old is Polly?
Eight going on sixteen.

Who do you think you are?
Lady Muck from Nannygoat Island?

ADVICE

Put some elbow grease into it.
Put your best foot forward.
Do it immediately if not sooner.
Don't bust your boiler.

You can't carry two watermelons under your arm.
Don't rock the boat.
Keep your nose to the grindstone.
That's as clear as mud.
DO·IT·YOURSELF

Rooster today, feather duster tomorrow.

Fools' names, like their faces,
Always appear in public places.

Good, better, best,
Never let it rest,
Till your good is better
And your better best.

Don't talk through
your hat.

Don't look at me in that tone of voice.

Tell tale tit,
Your tongue shall be split,
And all the little puppy dogs
Shall have a little bit.

Tell the truth and shame the Devil.

Don't let the cat
out of the bag.

See a pin and pick it up,
All the day you'll have good luck.
See a pin and let it lie,
You'll be sorry by and by.

It is a sin
To steal a pin,
Much more to steal
A greater thing.

Don't spit in the bowl in case you have to lick it out.
Satan makes work for idle hands to do.

Stop fussing —
you're buzzing around
like a blowfly in a pickle bottle.

Never say die till a dead
horse kicks you.

BED-TIME

Hit the sack.
Good night, sleep tight,
Mind the fleas don't bite.
If they do
Squeeze them tight.

Stella stellina,
The night's coming nearer
The star's winking bright;
The cow's in the barn,
Her calf's safe from harm;
The lamb's with the sheep,
The chicks are asleep.
Good night, good night.

Wake up, Australia!
7:00

Index